BUDDHIST
SCRIPTURES

BUDDHIST
SCRIPTURES

VIKING
an imprint of
PENGUIN BOOKS

Striving to understand the truth of the human
condition and following the path of spiritual
enlightenment is the fundamental nature of
Buddhism. Lighting this path is Buddha, meaning
Awakened One, Enlightened One. The Buddha
is not so much a single deity, but rather a
representation of a lineage of exemplars, or
enlightened disciples, committed to guiding
human beings to pure and happy lives.
Traditionally, Buddhists follow the teachings
of the historical Buddha, named Siddhartha
Gautama (sixth century BC, India). His teachings
have transpired through two main Buddhist
streams: Theravada ('way of the elders') and
Mahayana ('great vehicle').

The core sacred text of Theravada Buddhism
is the Tipitaka (also known as the Pali Canon
because the text is written in the ancient Indian
language of Pali). Tipitaka literally means 'three
baskets'. The sacred text was initially recorded

on dried palm leaves which were stored in three woven baskets, each one containing a different collection of teachings. The first is the Vinaya Pitaka, comprising monastic rules. The second is the Sutta Pitaka, which contains discourses of key Buddhist teachings, featuring the 'Four Noble Truths' and the 'Noble Eightfold Path'. The third and final collection of teachings is the Abhidhamma Pitaka, which means 'basket of higher teaching', a presentation of early philosophical treatises.

Within the Sutta Pitaka is the widely read Dhammapada, comprising verses that offer guidance towards the path to enlightenment. There is also the Jatakas, which is a collection of histories of the Buddha's past lives, each one teaching basic Buddhist values.

Mahayana Buddhism follows another collection of sacred texts, referred to as 'sutras' (or 'suttas'). Most of these contain the words of the Buddha's speeches to his followers and bodhisattvas.

An extension of Mahayana Buddhism is Tibetan Buddhism, or Tantrayana, which combines Mahayana and Tantric beliefs in a series of sacred texts called 'Tantras'. These are divided between two main collections of Indian Buddhist writings, called the Kanjur ('Translated Word of the Buddha') and the Tenjur ('treatises').

Unlike the world's other significant religions, Buddhism is non-theistic, driven simply by the Teachings of Buddha (the dhamma). Essentially, regardless of the variation of perspectives between Theravada and Mahayana, Buddhism is about identifying and exploring the nature of human suffering and providing resolutions of escape from it – the ultimate journey to enlightenment.

The following collection represents various Buddhist teachings, quotes and commentaries translated from and inspired by canonical Buddhist texts. Variation in the spelling of some terms may differ between Sanskrit and Pali languages.

The Four Noble Truths

The Truth of Suffering prescribes that life
is full of dhukkha (suffering);

The Truth of the Cause attributes this affliction
to notions of desire and ignorance;

If we remove this desire and ignorance,
we discover the Truth of Cessation;

It is only then, between the extremes
of asceticism and indulgence, that we learn
the Truth of the Way.

∽

Sutta Pitaka: Pali Canon

1

The Noble Eightfold Path

To discover the Truth of the Way (one of the
Four Noble Truths) one must subscribe to:

Right understanding – knowledge of the
Buddha's teachings.

Right resolve – good will in thought.

Right speech – speaking kindly (without lies).

Right conduct – caring actions (without harm).

Right livelihood – earning a living
without harming others.

Right effort – working hard to do good.

Right mindfulness – thinking before speaking or acting.

Right concentration – meditating to achieve mental calm.

Sutta Pitaka

There is a realm that is not earth, nor water, nor fire, nor air. It is not this world, nor the other world, neither the sun nor the moon. It does not come by birth, nor does it go by death. It is simply the end of suffering.

꩜

Sutta Pitaka

Do what is good, not what is evil.

Be pure of mind.

This is the teaching of the Buddha.

Dhammapada

This Pure Land is prosperous, comfortable

and fertile, for the pleasure of its many

gods and men. There is no hell.

There are no animals, nor ghosts.

Rich in flora and decorated with jewelled

trees, this is the Pure Land.

Pure Land Sutra

This is my simple religion. There is no
need for temples; no need for complicated
philosophy. Our own brain, our own heart
is our temple; the philosophy is kindness.

Tenzin Gyatso

the 14th Dalai Lama

Everything I see and hear is teaching me the path to follow. The flowing river teaches me that nothing lasts for ever . . . I do not need books made of paper and ink. Everything around me teaches me the dhamma.

∽

The Songs of Milarepa

Tibetan Buddhist scriptures

7

The Metta Sutta

Let all beings find happiness

Let hearts be whole.

Whatever beings they are –

Whether strong or weak,

Tall or short,

Small or large,

Beings seen or unseen,

Those living near or far away,

Those born,

And those yet to be born.

Let all of us find happiness.

∽

Sutta Pitaka

The mind paves the way for its objects.

To speak or act with a peaceful mind

brings happiness after oneself.

Dhammapada

9

Bodhisattvas practise generosity independent

of any object. Through this act of generosity,

without reliance on any form or concept, the

happiness that results is as infinite as space.

It cannot be measured.

Diamond Sutra

Avoid imbalance of the mind.

There will be praise and there will be blame.

Do not let either affect the poise of the mind:

Extinguish pride, follow calmness.

Sutta Nipata

Occasions of hatred are resolved by freedom

from hatred. This is the eternal law.

Dhammapada

Triumph over anger with love.

Triumph over evil with goodness.

Triumph over malice with generosity.

Triumph over lies with the truth.

Dhammapada

Let your love penetrate the universe,

To its great heights and depths,

A limitless love, free from hatred and hostility

Whether standing or walking, seated or lying down

As long as you are awake

Your life will bring heaven to earth.

Sutta Nipata

Old friends pass away, new friends appear.
It is just like the days. An old day passes,
a new day arrives. The important thing
is to make it meaningful: a meaningful
friend – or a meaningful day.

Tenzin Gyatso
the 14th Dalai Lama

15

Just as painful as an association

with unloved objects is a separation

from the objects that we love.

༤

Dhammapada

The wise follow concepts of common sense;

fools follow only hunger.

∽

Moral idea presented in the Jatakas

The Whatnot Tree

17

Because their minds are unobstructed they
are without fear. They have completely
passed beyond all error and so go on
to the fulfillment of nirvana.

Heart of Perfect Wisdom Sutra

The fool believes the battle is won with harsh speech, but finding forbearance alone brings one victory.

Samyutta Nikaya

19

To understand the principle of cause and effect – this being the result of that – is to rid one's self of bad views. Unspoiled, one abandons desire, fallacy and hatred, and acquires nirvana.

Nagarjuna

Second-century Indian scholar and writer
Founder of the Madhyamaka school of Indian Mahayana

20

A parent's kindness to his child is a virtue;

boundless and limitless.

Repaying that kindness is difficult

if one is irreverent.

Filial Piety Sutra

I will defend the defenseless; I will lead those who journey; I will be the boat, or bridge, or passage for those seeking the further shore.

Shantideva

Seventh-century Indian Buddhist

Through an attitude of giving to all beings –

of giving all of our possessions with their

fruits – a perfection of giving occurs;

it is essentially about attitude.

Shantideva

Seventh-century Indian Buddhist

23

Women are to be honoured

Women are heaven and they are truth

Women are Buddha, women are religion

Women are the perfection of wisdom.

༄

Chandamaharoshana Tantra

The Enlightened One is neither existence nor

non-existence; he has form, with face and body,

but in highest bliss he is formless.

ༀ

Hevajra Tantra

To know our body as foam, and to see

its qualities as a mirage, will free us from

the bonds of Mara.

Dhammapada

For those who understand that the
teaching of dhamma is like a raft,
dhamma should be abandoned.

∽

Diamond Sutra

The childish pursue their own self interests,

while the Able One chases the welfare of others.

Shantideva

Seventh-century Indian Buddhist

28

For the benefit of the entire world, bodhisattvas will dwell in suchness. They will establish all sentient beings in suchness and thereby lead them to nirvana.

Perfection of Wisdom Sutra

Innate is the world; its essence is innate

Its essence is also nirvana, with the mind

at its most pure.

Hevajra Tantra

The Path is fostered by the Buddhas
and Bodhisattvas awakened by the Eight Truths:

The world is impermanent.

Desire brings pain.

The more our minds are satisfied, the more we want.

Inactivity and self-indulgence lead us to downfall.

Ignorance causes death and rebirth.

Suffering through poverty creates conflict and ill-will.

Desire brings grief.

Birth and death give rise to suffering and affliction.

∽

Eight Enlightenment Sutra

Those who, through personal suffering,

aspire to end completely the suffering of all

others are persons of supreme capacity.

~

Atisha Dipamkara

Eleventh-century Indian Buddhist scholar and teacher

By refusing to harm others,

the good heart conquers all.

~

Moral idea presented in the Jatakas

King Goodness the Great

As human beings we all want to be happy and free from misery . . . we have learned that the key to happiness is inner peace. The greatest obstacles to inner peace are disturbing emotions such as anger and attachment, fear and suspicion, while love, compassion and a sense of universal responsibility are the sources of peace and happiness.

Tenzin Gyatso

the 14th Dalai Lama

34

Make friends with solitude and awaken
to the sweetness of tranquility. It will free
you from fear and misconduct. Then you
will taste the sweetness of truth.

Sutta Nipata

Penetrate your mind without fervour or attachment

Or be imprisoned by the evils of desire.

The Songs of Milarepa

Tibetan Buddhist scriptures

The ill-directed mind inflicts more harm

on one's self than an enemy or a hater.

Dhammapada

Understand the essence of the mind

Acknowledge that worries and disturbing

thoughts are engineered by the mind.

The Songs of Milarepa

Tibetan Buddhist scriptures

38

See the world as a bubble, a mirage

Then you will escape the eyes of Mara

See the world as a painted royal carriage

A trap for the fool

While those who understand it,

free from attachment, go free.

Dhammapada

Wisdom of the heart extinguishes ignorance and gives rise to knowledge, like a light that dispels darkness so that we may see objects clearly. It is the legacy of the Noble Truths.

Milindapañha

40

To develop and practise the perception of impermanence (of all beings); to remove all sensual passion and attachment to material existence; means to dismiss all ignorance and the conceit of 'I am.'

Samyutta Nikaya

Lust, hate and delusion

are the three roots of evil.

cs

Itivuttaka

42

Do not think lightly of evil, thinking it will pass you by. For just as a water pitcher fills up with every fall of a water drop, an unwise person accumulates evil, little by little.

Do not think lightly of goodness, thinking it will pass you by. For just as a water pitcher fills up with every fall of a water drop, a wise person accumulates goodness, little by little.

ᔐ

Dhammapada

The Four Immeasurables

May all sentient beings have equanimity,
free from attachment, aggression and prejudice.

May they be happy and find the cause
for happiness.

May they be free from suffering and
the cause of suffering.

May they never be separated from the
happiness that is free from suffering.

Tibetan prayer

The good person executes good deeds

with great ease

But the evil one finds it difficult.

The evil person executes evil deeds

with great ease

But the good one finds it difficult.

∽

Udana

45

To have faith we rely on practice

To have wisdom we must know the truth

Faith is the prerequisite of wisdom.

～

Nagarjuna

Second-century Indian scholar and writer
Founder of the Madhyamaka school of Indian Mahayana

46

Free from attachment to existence,

we are unrestrained; and so the

Path becomes clear.

∽

The Sutra of Hui Neng

Liberate the mind from the unripe;

this is the first step towards the ripening.

 ⌒

Anguttara Nikaya

A fool who lacks understanding

is his own worst enemy;

committing evil deeds

that bring bitter penalties.

∽

Dhammapada

A true Brahmana is free from desire.

He has discarded evil and impurity.

He is humble and self restrained,

knowledgeable and committed to holy life.

Udana

Like senseless children we are injured by suffering but love its causes. If our suffering is self-inflicted then why make others the object of our anger?

~

Shantideva

Seventh-century Indian Buddhist

51

Goodness flourishes with giving

Hatred compounds with restraint

By abandoning evil and dispelling

greed and hate, nirvana is gained.

Digha Nikaya

Reciting few sacred texts does not matter so much if one is committed to the practise of the Dhamma. By abandoning hatred and delusion, with wisdom and an unfettered mind, one can taste the blessings of a holy life.

~

Dhammapada

53

The relinquishing of all views

leads to emptiness

But if emptiness is the view,

then you have achieved nothing.

Nagarjuna

Second-century Indian scholar and writer
Founder of the Madhyamaka school of Indian Mahayana

54

A fool claims his children and his wealth
as his being. If he does not call himself
his own, how can he claim his children
and his wealth as his own?

༄

Dhammapada

Seek awakening by overcoming the insignificant

thoughts that can distract the mind.

Udana

To attain merit and virtue, ten Great and
Profound Vows should be carried out:

Pay tribute to and respect all Buddhas.
Honour the Thus Come Ones.
Make generous offerings.
Repent of and conquer karmic obstacles.
Rejoice in all merits and virtues.
Proclaim the doctrine of the Buddhas to the
world (turn the dhamma wheel).
Request that Buddhas remain in the world.
Always study with the Buddhas.
Be in harmony with all living beings.
Transfer all merit and virtue.

—

Avatamsaka Sutra
Flower Adornment Sutra

57

Dependence brings instability.

Relinquishing dependence brings

freedom from instability;

Which, in turn, brings peacefulness

and freedom from desire;

Then there is no coming and going and,

therefore, no birth or death.

With neither this world, nor that world,

we can celebrate the end of sorrow.

Udana

58

Understanding suffering and its cause,

and knowing the cessation of suffering and

how to achieve it, is called the Right View.

Digha Nikaya

Do good with urgency. If you are slow,

the mind too easily delights in evil.

❧

Dhammapada

A single possession on its own is enough

to keep the mind from discovering freedom.

∽

Moral idea presented in the Jatakas

The Shovel Wise Man

Generosity cultivates life, strength, beauty,
wit and ease. The giver participates in each of
these qualities, both in heaven and among men.

༄

Anguttara Nikaya

How does one subdue hostility

which is so vast?

Conquer the angry mind and every

rival becomes a friend.

Shantideva

Seventh-century Indian Buddhist

Speak without harm or ill-will to others.

Practise moderation in food and

peacefulness in seclusion.

Devote yourself to higher consciousness.

This is the teaching of the Buddhas.

∽

Dhammapada

The Five Precepts

I undertake the precept to refrain from
destroying living creatures.
I undertake the precept to refrain from taking
that which is not given.
I undertake the precept to refrain from
sexual misconduct.
I undertake the precept to refrain
from incorrect speech.
I undertake the precept to refrain from intoxicating
liquors and drugs which lead to carelessness.

These Five Precepts have morality as a vehicle for
happiness; they have morality as a vehicle for good
fortune; they have morality as a vehicle for
liberation. Let morality, therefore, be purified.

༃

Theravada prayer

One dispels gossip by abandoning it.

One speaks rightly in time and in fact,

on the Dhamma and its disciplines. These are

words worth recording, words that are

reasonable, moderate and beneficial.

Majjhima Nikaya

66

He who finds fault with others is himself
in the wrong. With earnest, tread the path
and see not the mistakes of the world.

∽

The Sutra of Hui Neng

Like a beautiful brightly coloured

flower without fragrance

Is the well-spoken word without action.

Like a beautiful brightly coloured

flower full of fragrance

Is the well-spoken word and the deed

that matches the word.

∽

Dhammapada

We can never obtain peace in the outer world

until we make peace with ourselves.

~

Tenzin Gyatso

the 14th Dalai Lama

The nature of the Buddha realm of 'bliss'

originates from those sentient beings that,

in this realm of bliss, are free from physical

and mental anguish. Instead they encompass

pure joy and happiness.

cɔ

The Smaller Pure Land Sutra

The ten acts of kindness a mother
bestows on her child are:

Providing protection in the womb.
Bearing the physical pain of childbirth.
Forgetting the physical pain of childbirth
once the child is born.
Eating the bitter to save the sweet for the child.
Lying in the wet to move the child into the dry.
Nurturing the child at her breast.
Washing away the unclean.
Thinking of the child, whether it is close
to home or afar.
Ardent care and devotion.
Ultimate pity and sympathy.

᠊ᠥ

Filial Piety Sutra

Like a fish out of water, the mind quavers

when it breaks free from the control of Mara.

ॐ

Dhammapada

Associate with the wise, not with fools.

Honour those who are deserved of honour.

Sutta Nipata

Be mindful and you will find immortality;

Be ignorant and you will find death.

The wise rejoice in mindfulness;

Through meditation they will reach nirvana.

Dhammapada

From the head to the feet, everything dissolves

into your heart; you engage in the supreme

state of meditation (on emptiness).

Guhyasamaja Tantra

75

A fool is happy

Until his mischief turns against him.

And a good man may suffer

Until his goodness flowers.

Dhammapada

Let there be nothing behind you;
leave the future to one side. Do not clutch
at what is left in the middle; then you will
become a wanderer and calm.

Sutta Nipata

There is no meditative concentration for
one who lacks wisdom, and no wisdom for one
lacks meditative concentration. One in whom
are found both meditative concentration and
wisdom is indeed close to nirvana.

⌒

Dhammapada

Right speech, harmlessness,

Restraint in speaking ill of others,

Moderation in food, at peace in

remoteness and solitude,

Devotion to higher meditation.

This is the teaching of the Buddhas.

∽

Dhammapada

The animals had placed themselves in grave danger because they had listened to rumours and unsubstantiated fears rather than seeking out the truth for themselves.

∽

Duddubha Jataka

By amending our mistakes, we get wisdom.

By defending our faults, we betray an

unsound mind.

༄

The Sutra of Hui Neng

Where there is dependence, there is instability, where there is no dependence, there is no instability, where there is no instability, there is quietude, where there is quietude, there is no desire, where there is no desire, there is no coming or going, where there is no coming or going, there is no birth or death, where there is no birth or death, there is neither this world or that world, nor both: that is the end of sorrow.

Udana

82

Most people never realise that all
of us here shall one day perish.

But those who do realise that truth
settle their quarrels peacefully.

Dhammapada

Happy is he who lives contented in solitude,

is well-versed in the Doctrine and has

realised it. Happy is he who lives in this world

free from ill will, and is benevolent towards

all beings. Happy is he who lives in this

world free from passion, has overcome sensual

enjoyment, and has attained mastership

over the conceit of 'I am.' This indeed

is the highest happiness.

Udana

In whom there dwells no self-deception

and no pride,

Whose lust and selfishness are gone,

who is desireless,

Whose wrath is put away, whose

self hath cool become –

He is a brahmin, he [is] a recluse, he is a monk.

Udana

There is no fire like the fire of lust;

There is no sin like the sin of hatred;

There are no sufferings like the sufferings

of existence;

There is no happiness like Supreme Tranquility.

Dhammapada

86

By giving, merit grows,

by restraint, hatred's checked.

He who's skilled abandons evil things.

As greed, hate and folly wane,

nirvana's gained.

∽

Digha Nikaya

Although he recites many sacred texts,
if he does not act accordingly, that heedless
man is like a cowherd who only counts
the cattle of others – he does not partake
of the blessings of a holy life.

Although he recites few sacred texts,
if he puts the Dhamma into practice,
forsaking lust, hatred, and delusion, with true
wisdom and emancipated mind, clinging to
nothing in this or any other world – he,
indeed, partakes of the blessings of a holy life.

∽

Dhammapada

Just as a mother would protect with her life
her own son, her only son, so one should
cultivate an unbounded mind towards all beings,
and loving kindness towards all the world.

One should cultivate an unbounded mind,
above and below and across, without
obstruction, without enmity, without rivalry.

Standing, or going, or seated, or lying down,
as long as one is free from drowsiness,
one should practise this mindfulness.
This, they say, is the holy state here.

Sutta Nipata

Do not choose bad friends.

Do not choose persons of low habits.

Select good friends. Be discriminating.

Choose the best.

ᘓ

Dhammapada

One sees pleasure as suffering

And sees pain as a dart.

One sees as impermanent the peaceful feeling

That is neither pleasant nor painful.

Such a bhikkhu who sees rightly

Is thereby well released.

Accomplished in knowledge, at peace,

That sage has overcome all bonds.

Itivuttaka

91

Speak not harshly to anyone.

Those thus addressed will retort.

Painful, indeed, is vindictive speech.

Blows in exchange may bruise you.

If, like a cracked gong, you silence yourself,

you have already attained nirvana:

no vindictiveness will be found in you.

Dhammapada

Without realising the unity of Bliss and Void,

Even though on the Void you meditate,

You practise only Nihilism.

～

Hundred Thousand Songs of Milarepa

Greed, I say, is a great flood; it is a whirlpool

sucking one down, a constant yearning,

seeking a hold, continually in movement;

difficult to cross is the morass of sensual desire.

A sage does not deviate from truth,

a brahmana stands on firm ground;

renouncing all, he is truly called 'calmed'.

Sutta Nipata

When you observe your mind with penetration,

Stir not ardent passion or attachment

Lest the devil of desire possess you.

Son, rest at ease and without hope.

Hundred Thousand Songs of Milarepa

95

Victory produces hatred; he that is defeated

is afflicted with suffering;

He that has renounced both victory and defeat

lives in tranquility and happiness.

∽

Dhammapada

If you only believe that Buddha speaks no words,

Then the Lotus will blossom in your mouth.

The Sutra of Hui Neng

As sweet as honey, thinks a fool an evil deed,

so long as it bears no fruit;

But when it bears fruit,

then the fool comes to grief.

੭

Dhammapada

The fool who thinks he is a fool is for that

very reason a wise man;

But the fool who thinks he is a wise man

is rightly called a fool.

Dhammapada

99

Wisdom is but Self-awareness,

Beyond all words and talk.

↶

Hundred Thousand Songs of Milarepa

Nowhere.

Not in the sky,

Nor in the midst of the sea,

Nor deep in the mountains,

Can you hide from your own mischief.

Not in the sky,

Nor in the midst of the ocean,

Nor deep in the mountains,

Nowhere

Can you hide from your own death.

∾

Dhammapada

Now you have seen the true doctrine,

your guileless heart loves to exercise its

charity, for wealth and money are inconstant

treasures, 'twere better quickly to bestow

such things on others.

Fo-Sho-Hing-Tsan-King

Even as rain breaks through

an ill-thatched house,

So lust breaks through an ill-trained mind.

Even as rain breaks not through

a well-thatched house,

So lust breaks not through a well-trained mind.

༄

Dhammapada

Going along in company together, a wise man

Must mix with other foolish persons.

But on seeing what is wrongful

he abandons them.

As a full-fledged heron leaves

the marshy ground.

Udana

A sage does not speak in terms

of being equal, lower or higher.

Calmed and without selfishness

he neither grasps nor rejects.

Sutta Nipata

'Look how he abused me and beat me,
How he threw me down and robbed me.'
Live with such thoughts and you live in hate.

'Look how he abused me and beat me,
How he threw me down and robbed me.'
Abandon such thoughts and live in love.

In this world
Hate never yet dispelled hate.
Only love dispels hate.
This is the law,
Ancient and inexhaustible.

Dhammapada

Develop the mind of equilibrium. You will always

be getting praise and blame, but do not

let either affect the poise of the mind:

follow the calmness, the absence of pride.

Sutta Nipata

Where neither water nor yet earth

Nor fire nor air gain a foothold,

There gleam no stars, no sun sheds light,

There shines no moon, yet there

no darkness reigns.

When a sage, a Brahmin,

has come to know this

For himself through his own experience,

Then he is freed from form and formlessness,

Freed from pleasure and from pain.

Udana

For one who is in the habit of constantly

honouring and respecting the elders,

four blessings increase –

age, beauty, bliss, and strength.

᷐

Dhammapada

Trivial thoughts, insignificant thoughts,

When followed they distract the mind.

Not understanding those thoughts

The roaming mind runs back and forth.

But by understanding those thoughts

One ardent and mindful restrains the mind.

An awakened one has overcome

them completely

So they do not arise to distract the mind.

Udana

The best scenery is nought-to-see –

That is the Mind-Essence of Illumination.

Hundred Thousand Songs of Milarepa

III

Who would have thought that all things are

the manifestation of the Essence of Mind.

The Sutra of Hui Neng

112

A man who has but little, grows old like an ox;

His flesh increases, but his wisdom, not.

∽

Dhammapada

113

Our very nature is Buddha, and apart from this nature there is no other Buddha.

༄

The Sutra of Hui Neng

Nothing is born, nothing is destroyed.
Away with your dualism, your likes
and dislikes. Every single thing is just
the One Mind. When you have perceived this,
you will have mounted the Chariot
of the Buddhas.

Zen Teaching of Huang Po

You should know that so far as Buddha-nature

is concerned, there is no difference between

an enlightened man and an ignorant one.

What makes the difference is that one realises it,

while the other is ignorant of it.

The Sutra of Hui Neng

116

Glossary of Buddhist terms

Variation in the spelling of some terms may differ between Sanskrit and Pali languages.

Buddha
Enlightened one, awakened one – guiding us to nirvana.

Bodhisattvas
God-like beings that have attained enlightenment but have chosen to delay their entry into nirvana in order to help others; Avalokitesvara is the most popular of the bodhisattvas.

Dalai Lama
The temporal and spiritual leader of Tibet. 'Dalai' is Mongolian for 'Ocean', 'Lama' is Tibetan for 'high reincarnation' – together they mean 'Ocean of Wisdom.' Dalai Lamas are a succession of religious leaders belonging to the Gelug sect of Tibetan Buddhism. They are believed to be manifestations of the great Bodhisattva, Avalokitesvara. The current and 14th Dalai Lama is Tenzin Gyatso.

Dhamma
Teachings of the Buddha; doctrine of truth.

Dukkha
Unhappiness; suffering.

Mara
King of the Demons, of death.

Nirvana
A euphoric deathless state; ultimate reality reached through enlightenment. For Buddhists, this is the ultimate goal but it is difficult to positively characterise; the 'Fourfold Negation' is a supporting philosophical principle that deals with ideas of the nature of our existence (unconditioned existence).

Pali
Ancient Indian language, associated with Theravada scriptures.

Sanskrit
Ancient Indian language, associated with Mahayana scriptures.

Thus Come Ones
A reference to Buddha. 'Thus' implies stillness; 'Come' suggests action. Together the words connote stillness within action or vice versa.

Tipitaka
Sacred scriptures of Theravada Buddhists (also referred to as the Pali Canon).

Endnotes

List of prominent canonical Buddhist texts:

Tipitaka

~ Vinaya Pitaka

~ Sutta Pitaka

- ⌄ Digha Nikaya (the long collection)

- ⌄ Majjhima Nikaya (the middle-length collection)

- ⌄ Samyutta Nikaya (the grouped collection)

- ⌄ Anguttara Nikaya
  (the further-factored collection)

- ⌄ Khuddaka Nikaya (the collection of little texts):

  Khuddakapatha

  Dhammadapa

  Udana

  Itivuttaka

  Sutta Nipata

  Vimanavatthu

  Petavatthu

  Theragatha

  Therigatha

Jataka

Niddesa

Patisambhidamagga

Apadana

Buddhavamsa

Cariyapitaka

Nettippakarana
(in the Burmese Tipitaka only)

Petakopadesa

Milindapañha

෴ Abbhidhamma Pitaka

Mahayana Sutras

෴ Texts of Indian Origin:

⌄ Diamond Sutra

⌄ Heart Sutra

⌄ Lankavatara Sutra

⌄ Lotus Sutra

⌄ Perfection of Wisdom (Prajnaparamita) Sutras

⌄ Ten Stages Sutra

⌄ Vimalakirti-nirdesa Sutra

∽ Texts of Chinese Origin:

  ⌄ Platform Sutra (Liuzu Danjing)

  ⌄ Perfect Enlightenment Sutra (Yuanjue Jing)

VIKING

Published by the Penguin Group
Penguin Group (Australia)
250 Camberwell Road, Camberwell, Victoria 3124, Australia
(a division of Pearson Australia Group Pty Ltd)
Penguin Group (USA) Inc.
375 Hudson Street, New York, New York 10014, USA
Penguin Group (Canada)
10 Alcorn Avenue, Toronto, Ontario, Canada M4V 3B2
(a division of Pearson Penguin Canada Inc.)
Penguin Books Ltd
80 Strand, London WC2R 0RL, England
Penguin Ireland
25 St Stephen's Green, Dublin 2, Ireland
(a division of Penguin Books Ltd)
Penguin Books India Pvt Ltd
11 Community Centre, Panchsheel Park, New Delhi – 110 017, India
Penguin Group (NZ)
Cnr Airborne and Rosedale Roads, Albany, Auckland, New Zealand
(a division of Pearson New Zealand Ltd)
Penguin Books (South Africa) (Pty) Ltd
24 Sturdee Avenue, Rosebank, Johannesburg 2196, South Africa

Penguin Books Ltd, Registered Offices: 80 Strand, London, WC2R 0RL, England

First published by Penguin Group (Australia), a division of Pearson Australia Group Pty Ltd, 2005

10 9 8 7 6 5 4 3 2 1

Text selection copyright © Penguin Group (Australia) 2005

The moral right of the author has been asserted

Cover & text design by Adam Laszczuk © Penguin Group (Australia)
Cover photograph by Bridgeman Art Library
Cover background pattern by The Pepin Press / Agile Rabbit Editions
Printed in China by Bookbuilders

National Library or Australia
Cataloguing-in-Publication data:

Buddhist Scriptures.

ISBN 0 6700 2892 4.

1. Buddhism - Sacred books.
I. Title.

294.382

www.penguin.com.au